The Joy that Cracked the Mountain

THE JOY THAT CRACKED THE MOUNTAIN

PATRICK O'CONNELL

The Muses' Company Series Editor: Catherine Hunter
Cover design by Terry Gallager/Doowah Design Inc.
Cover photo by Patrick O'Connell
Author photo by Sandy Brown

Published with the financial assistance of The Canada Council for the Arts and the Manitoba Arts Council.

Printed and bound in Canada

Canadian Cataloguing in Publication Data

O'Connell, Patrick, 1944–
     The joy that cracked the mountain

ISBN 1-896239-52-8

     I. Title.

PS8579.C65J69 1999   C811'.54   C99-901011-5
PR9199.3.O36J69 1999

to Rod

Patrick O'Connell

For the partly wounded

CONTENTS

THE SPIRAL NOTEBOOK

Urge and urge and urge
always the procreant urge of the world

—Walt Whitman, *Song of Myself*

Somehow it never served me well
all that skin
          and ecstasy
that flesh that poured like honey
into the dark
so to the sound of one hand clapping
I'll embrace my bones
and drop the ragged bundle
of my want
the burning world
that bleeding fantasy
I used to drag along the hall/every smoky night

How I have inhabited this miracle
and go all the way to emptiness
on a night when the wind
blows a ghost up my sleeve
for it's almost as if I'd gotten past
the chaos of hunger and want
and arrived here in this one-horse town
trying to go the distance
with a cardboard suitcase
full of burning leaves
so you might say I'm interested
in something a little less frantic
than death or fantasy
not even sure I wanted all that sky
that bare bulb
that circus balloon that drifts past
my head.
or my ragged shoes with no laces
that the birds have flown away

For Leef Evans

It must be this Light coming through the crack
that keeps me asking
that keeps me yearning to be born

Hoping the dirt will burst into flowers
and that my hellfire words will sail through the air
as if they were spoken by bells

So quiet here you can hear the woodticks
landing on the cattle
and the hollow men on sidewalks/giving up the ghost

As I go waltzing the bear again
while the little wind-up soldier
is battering on his drum

No request nor expectation
only the vivid chaos of the year
and the shade the trees give off
to every saint and skeleton
thinking if I could bend
and perform the transformation
of just being here
in solidarity with the sky
while a dog nips at my heels
and a blue-bird flies right through
the eye of the needle
O look
the August leaves so dark now
they are almost black
here on the sandy ground where I wait
as if you were calling

For Sandy Brown

Like the crust of ice at the river's edge
I am half-way in and half-way out
of a wrecked season
where you might have heard me calling
along some cobbled alleyway
in the red-lipped blue-lipped city
where I have gone and dreamt 'til dawn
that all my hands were tangled in your hair

So I'm calling you now can you hear this
this is a singing telegram
where I've thrown the door wide open
for your rain
so come back to me like the time you did
when we wrestled as one
when the angel we never believed in
blew her golden horn
and a blue butterfly flew into the room
O how every moment we grew younger
with a phosphoresence on our skin
while a perfect wave crashed on a beach
to the sound of the harpsichord wind

For Arthur Adamson

So it was me going on and recurring again
in the space between the spaces
with a seagull in my mailbox
and a chart to lead me to the place
where I might die for beauty

As I turn to the gypsy darkness
and the thousand hallelujahs
of the wind
so just to let you know
the unspeakable wheel is turning
and every windswept phoenix has taken wing

For Gisela Gielow

I think the sultry sky just did a trick
hip as I am to the miracle of air
and this thing that ticks in my shirt

When all I ever wanted was a moment's self-possession
to come up to the newborn
with a forty-year amen
astonished by the murmur on my skin

O long past the idiot pleasure
and all the shabby trinkets of the world
where I'll die singing like Willy Blake
and blow a farewell kiss

And not confuse the raven, with the night

For Chetan Rajani

It might have been the day
I walked out on the world
the world and its ten thousand joys
its ten thousand sorrows
tip-toeing along the highway in my glass shoes
where it's always the same question
the simple art of being here
accepting the long shadow that I cast
and reeling myself in
as if my heart were a crow on a string
and I'd gone by the blistered
up forty floors of stairs
trying to speak the mixed-up names
of all the baffled dead
so don't look to me for mere decorations
or anything to divert you from
ruthless Heaven or the ruthless Earth

For Margaret Wiens

Two bluejays landed on our branch
a breeze blew a kind of texture on the river
cottonwood leaves rustled like chimes
and while your one-year-old waved her spoon in the air
I wanted to tell you everything
how I had extinguished all desire
though I ate the salad hungrily
and must have revealed my want I guess
by the way I looked at you
a sight for sore eyes in your red boots
but sensing that all our grace lies in our control
I simply laughed and blinked
like my old aunt on a holiday from the bank
who would never reveals the contents of her soul

For Rose Moodrey

It was only a way of holding oneself
to take the risk and hear the wind
to wreck the horn of plenty
though I think that was before the Fall
when I had arced like a haunted heart
across the startled heavens
dreaming the delirious sky again
when it all came back to a twilight room
with the scent of rain in the window
and a bird who flew out of a smoky mirror
so I felt the rush of being there
and the ecstasy of knowing what I knew
the prayer that staggered from my lips
world without end then
when the only choice I had/was to sing

For the Unknown Soldier

You could call this a prayer for a man on a wheel
for one who goes pleading with the night
who finds no answer yet finds an answer
in the emptiness of halls
and turns back to where he came from
some November asylum in his summer shirt
there on the edge of oblivion
somehow wounded by beauty and the tortured light
with a rusty cannon in his burlap sack
and two bones he clacks every night
O every night he sings the same old story
leaning there against a burning door

It's only the world and its horror and beauty
a film unfurling inside your head
as you stagger into the pentecost
hoping for the Light to guide you
home like a hummingbird
only to wind up in a shack for rent
with thirty-six bottles of Triple-X
and a man rolled up in a rug
like a rebellious bride in a cottonwood tree
who is climbing towards her wisdom now
all caught up in her veil
so it's the blues I guess for sandmen eh
and all of us looking along the shore
amongst the bric-a-brac and bloated fish
for a blizzard to start its engine in our soul

For Janine Legal

Here on the collapsing ramparts
where I've been for forty moons
while yellow leaves like death on wheels
clack along the avenue
where the digger's done and Christ comes empty
and I feel like some old night machine
that lost its driving wheel
while the pie in the sky explodes
and the captain in his tinfoil suit
goes up and down the snakes and ladders
trying to salvage what he can
while I'm still here doing a can-can dance
as the owl in the graveyard flies through my shoes

For Stephen Riley

I had crawled out of a grave somewhere
and danced a jig beside that smoking hole
I Lazarus
who went back to the house where I was born
where rain stung like needles on my skin
where I met with those with bangles on their wrists
those swarthy Gypsies with far-away eyes
who took me with them in their colored caravans
after I had spoken/with a kind of majesty
about every flower that ever bloomed and fell

For Robyn Maharaj

OK it was the eloquent dark

and the confabulations of a mind
that somehow passed on sorrow
and revelled there in its prayer
and its penniless boots
while the white magnolia
shifted in its vase
and I saw my face
there in the grain of the wood
while time ticked like an iron thing
that was coming all apart

And struck by the impermanence of things
I am called to that which never lasts
yet go on this joyous errand
as if I had wings

O it's a kind of hallelujah
that I am trying to stutter on the road

How I am everywhere and here
in this amazing winter
striving for a perfect kind
of poverty
for an emptiness that might ring
like a bell

And now this voice again
as if there were leaves in the mind
when time is short and time is long
and the nightwind's hands are true

So it's the winding stairway then
two steps at a time
where later tonight
I will remember the world
the way it is a full-page want-ad
going up in smoke

For David Scott

I've seen my ragged reflection in every downtown window
in every spring pool by roadsides where I've been

Concealing my grief
and hauling myself across the boneyards of high noon

Though man it was swell when the moon rose
over the crippled city

And I thought there was a wild bird in my throat

For Billie Holiday

Now what about your Christlike feet
or your mind like a snowblind thing
flying right past the edge

For what you contain is a multitude
somehow concealed by a veil
and the most beautiful thing you ever did
was ask

About those acts of mutiny
you performed in an empty room
standing on that bamboo chair
and calling out forever

While the night bloomed in your hair
which you couldn't see for all the smoke
that rose like birds from a highway

The cracked mirror you threw in the swamp
and your heart that wore itself out
begging for Light in the rain

Here on the edge with a moth in my slipper
trying to forget and trying to remember
the nightwind in my hair

So this is for the light and the dark
for the heron on one leg
standing by the edge of the river

Where the August sun
burns right through my flowered vest
speaking the prayer you taught me once
when I was falling from a pier

Making a few extra bucks doing handstands
on the crumpled edge of the wreck

For Samuel Beckett

I was trying to figure my way through the darkness
every once-in-awhile there was a tree
every once-in-awhile
there was a memory
but I want you to know from the depth of my being
I went on I went on
past the stumbling drifters and the bar belles
I was like a man with a magic hand
who headed toward the sanctuary of his being
and if I died and died again
on that collapsible stretcher
It's true I sang as pure as any bird

For Patrick Friesen

When it was all that you had striven for
knowing there is no difference
between the diamond and the dust
as you go through the moonlit archway
with a kind of worship in your soul
pulling a bird from your sleeve
because you were born to roll
across the old mythology
with starshine on your windshield
where you lived to tell the wounded
about the furious Light
when you held the Vision for a moment
in a dream you had one night
and begged the grace to call you by your name

For Alexandra Karacsony

It was just a reflection on a glass
your heroic beauty
and all the tricks your heart knows
to get you through the night
like the gratitude you feel
for your own tiny garden
for skin and the moon that climbs
like a swimming girl
to the gracious rhythm
of someone's gorgeous hands upon
a cello
O like a seashell empty of all things
you just know and know

For Maggie Dwyer

It's the thing you held most dear to you
what you called an emptiness
or a genuflection
having made your bargain with the oval night
with the shuttle and the darkness
of your loom
and the way you were startled by the brittle air
when it all came back to you
what you called a song from a room
while you did a perfect pirouette
before a mirror
when a whole new language
when another way of reckoning appeared
deep inside the crevice of your knowing
O turn turn and turn again
were the words you wrote on the sky

Boz and Molly
(A Romance)

Wine can endow the lowest dive
with sudden luxury

— Baudelaire

The two of us together here
sprawled inside some cardboard box
that tumbles through the sky

Homeless then in the infernal air
while children in the street
perform their merry executions
with paper swords

O the god that marches through our night
like a dark wind
so use the word wrench/use the word oblivion

O what the hell did we ever achieve
except a goddamn rum run
in the rain

Or a long waltz through a boneyard
where you coughed your venom
into me

Where we staggered toward the season
of our birth
and knew about the blacksmith in our brain

And went strewing broken birds
down a cobbled lane

Shuddering there, we are each other's fiends
joined at the loins while all the birds of the world
revolve through our burning dream

And later that wine will rush through our skin
and we'll cry at the selves that we have been
bastards on the road in the muscatel wind
where we crush all the violent flowers

And go toward the night as if we knew
something about that wheel we are attached to
that rolls like some old engine into hell

Our house with a barbed-wire fence
with a skull on the gate
while I hang up all those TB sheets
on a creaking line
and the mailman with his pepper-spray
knocking out our dog
while you fry bones in an iron pot
and the house is full of fog

O just to let you know
our submarine came in
and Bacchus is running naked through our ruins

Consider us in a farther field
chained to the dark while we seek our resolution
by bending horseshoes into figure-eights
and dusting off the artificial rose
then drag that circus cart through ruts
when the sky is black with the wings of crows

And we could read between the lines
between the wine and the hysteria
and called out to the Jackal with his bone
saying we were half-way through the darkness now
dreaming rabid bites
while some snake shed its skin on our concrete floor

And us coming on like floodlights
having placed the bingo sign
at the feet of the plaster Saviour
the sun going down like a junkie, waving his last dime

I wonder what I could do in the face of this death
maybe light some incense
or throw a burning lily onto the road

O remember the shroud the dead sailor was in
when they let him slide into the sea

It's just the way the heart goes on sometimes
rustling as if it were leaves and leaves

And you in that church in the rain one night
when you just lay down on the altar

O one time in some port-town
with a seahorse in your hair
you made a bee-line for your innocence
and totally loved a guy

And now that you're in the darkness
you remember the light
speaking words about a highway
and someone's goddamn rooster
right inside your hat

While you're hauling ass through limbo
trying like hell to reach the rope
that is tied to a get-away

Just hear this woman's story
hear her story
you can hear it all on the wind
the way she says yes, the way she says no
to her burden
and some nights it is so certain
the stove will click
and she'll kick her shoes across the floor
while the burning world goes rolling by
just outside our curtains

Coughing up our ecstasy
while we hear some ancient torch song
in our blood

Some nights, we are one
the way the sky and wind are
or a blackened cauldron
full of snow

And call that thing that shrieks
and shrieks
the kind of love we know

While you dance and rant
for the crescent moon
under the deer-crossing sign
with its seven bullet holes

You talked about the hum of the fridge
as the basic fact of our existence
and your rise and fall and ecstasy
when you were queen sorrow just for a day
when you wore that feathered-boa and netted stockings
while we waltzed right past the setting sun
past the junkyard and the gleaming shanty-town
and then along the burning highway of our love

I have gone through winter streets
and murdered time
with something deep inside me
that I could not name

So it's the chaos of not knowing
and the ship that sinks in my drink
though I've built a little bridge to you
and have gone across the silent scream
of every night
and landed there like I had wings
and knew which way to yearn

Though every time I looked behind
things were toppling
still, I went on
past all the smoking manholes in the world

I feel for you there, out on a limb
with that corpse you are always carrying
for my heart too
spins like a wheel
and I must have spent a lifetime
as you have
riding toward the country of the dead
trying to appease the ghost of love
with a shot or two of gin
funny eh, how we never win
on the inside, a way down deep in our bones

I dreamed my car had four flat tires
that my fingers had turned into cigarettes
which were smoking me

And later the wine and cheese party
without the cheese

O there are some dark things in the night my dear
like climbing the wall for a drink
dying over and over in the kitchen sink
and running out of matches
when you're trying to burn the shit-box down

When Hurricane Mitch the son of a bitch
blew all our laundry away

We could hear the rats gallop in
though there was going to be some whiskey
there was going to be the mercy of a yell

While we did that one-armed butcher's reel
across a smoking rug
and felt the night air rushing on our shins

Having paid our rent with empties
and a pail of shattered glass
we go toward the exit sign in scorched shoes

It was just the eternal banging of the wind
and us going on with our hillbilly hymn
and then a long rant about that highway
that rolls right past our bed
like the night I saw your face appear
in the crucifixion
and us coming on like worn out dice
friends, let's just say we died there
leaning out of windows
trying to trace the shape of an O in the sky.

Maybe this is the end of love
maybe you could call this
the Xeroxed end
the thing that goes in hobnail boots
across our electric souls
while we wag and wag and wag again
and then hear it all snap
like the twist-off cap/on some cheap Canadian red

We'll make it past the riff raff
and the creaking gate
and pour a forty-ouncer
on old Delaney's grave
he who stayed sober in Seattle
for nearly a month
until the lightning hit his stuff
and thirteen engines pounded
in his brain

I remember the night you murdered me
when you tore the skin right off my back
and went backwards along the flamingo yard
with a cannonball stuffed in your shirt

And later I resurrect like some old soldier
while you drink a scotch on that chesterfield
we bought on a lay-away plan

Hoping Jesus
hoping Jesus going to be here soon

Like a monk without a cloister
or a lover with no arms
I bounced off the walls all night
while seagulls landed in the yard

Not to mention
the barnacles on my feet
or that beast I dragged up from the deep
that is beating its wings in my hair

I loved you then
when you rolled that rusted dream machine
down the tortured hall
with a Morning Glory in your hair
when the convoluted sky
let out a scream

While I mouthed your fine skin
and then all of me
drifted away like leaves

And we were just two fragments there
remnants from some hungry house
while the hands of the plaster Saviour
caught the rain

THE JOY THAT CRACKED THE MOUNTAIN

Joy & Woe are woven fine
A Clothing for the Soul divine
Under every grief and pine
Runs a joy with silken twine

— William Blake

I just walked in out of the blue and was
wondering what I knew about this colossal
mystery. The truth in trees that bloom
without a sound and the heart's deep blue
crescendo. O here where I dream that I'm
right here, beginning to perceive the
wonder. Like that summer when we went with
swimmer's legs and swimmer's arms and
flowers in a garden. And went head-over-heels
in our glad-rags into the speckled dark.

Here where I've bloomed and died and bloomed
again. Where the way is always vertical and
I climb. For it's how I conceive of the
world.
　　　The way the night sighs like leaves
when my coat makes a sail for the wind. So
it's spring rain and a violin. And two girls
dancing along the road. Throwing their arms
at the sky. While the night goes on forever
like a turning carousel
and I hear the far-off echo
of my name.

So it's starlight saving time and a night
in a Spanish garden. In gold-spangled shoes
and dark greens and blues, I'm working my
diamond machine. And coming up empty of
everything except the radiance of the mind.
Where I go the way the lightning did, with
a sparrow in my vest. Here, where I call
my death a birth, I break free of the old
cocoon. So when all those faithless hearts
are being swallowed by the shadows
I'll openup the windows for the moon.

O now that I've mastered my past and
extinguished doubt and bought a one-way
ticket to freedom from a blind angel in
a boat. And though the sky is down and
out, I'm making waves with a chant.
I'm belly-dancing right through your yard
and shouting to the world that my madness
is divine. I'm going last and I'm going
first. A man with a handful of lilacs
who can barely make it through his window
for all the nightingales.

It always was a matter of suffering and
transcendence. Of waiting for the heart
to sing. When I knew the night was just
the thing I'd always longed for. And
carved a hole out of the darkness for the
ghost of all my leaves.
As I talk about my karmic debt and how I
loved a woman. So call it a going home.
Call it a pilgrimage. The way we lay our
bodies down, just to hear the rain.

It's what the memory had shaped, as if the
memory had a mind of its own. So pain and
longing were soon forgotten. But not the
perception that rain is blue. So I've taken
no oath. I've sworn to nothing. But a long
siesta and a drink of the cool earth. Where
I'm taking all my signals from the burnished
sky and will sail across the hardwood floor
as if I was a schooner in bloom.

There on some summer bridge, in shirtsleeves
with a diamond brooch, I'm waiting for the
night light on the river. Where I hear the
silence deepen and dream a chant I've heard.
So later tonight, with no expectation, I'll go
right through the perfumed void and echo all
those songbirds in the hall. Where I'll burn
the nights like firewood and somehow speak
your name.

O earth allow my praise and let my heart
be the thing that keeps me crossing this
stubble field at twilight and high noon.
As I come to you now under the most uncanny
sky with wide open arms and a tattoo of a
bluebird on my wrist. And there was no
turning back once the night touched on your
sleeve. Once your potter's wheel started
creaking.

It was toward a thing that turned, the way I
went, and found myself drawn to the water. Or
more precisely, to the light within the water
that I cupped within my hands. O if I could cough
my name up and somehow embrace this diamond
I might be wise enough to know there is a path
that winds its way right through hell. When
we've been true as trees and laid a naked kiss
upon the thorn.

Thus the vision bloomed in me and I became
a sandman whose sandals left tracks along
a starving road. Now the circular thing
the heart goes through when you beg the light
to stay. When time burns slowly, like an
incense stick. When some native youth, in
a midnight street, makes the cry of a loon.
So in a lot of ways we're like the birds
the way we gather and disperse and call the
night our own.

An oddity, in that he never believed, but
always was a worshipper. For it was only
human decency just to bow. To know the
mind and call a light a light. And
glorious was the river that flowed through
the darkness of his soul. And like a
baby's cry on a windy street, he sometimes
grieved but asked for nothing. But just
went on in his second-hand suit, knowing
it is loving that leads to love and all things
pass quickly away. A diamond cutter like
no other, free and easy on the open road
while the bells of Saint Mary's rang.

I'll call it fine, this face I kissed, while
all the yellow tulips yawned in the yard.
For I am a witness, writing on leaves and
I'm singing a hymn to the universe. And if
you listen long enough you will hear my
harmony. For is the space between heaven
and earth not shaped like a hand.

I'm writing to tell you I made it over
the wall and crossed a summer field at
dawn, startling white birds into the air.
O could you ever believe in a heart that
never danced. Hallucinating minstrel
with a diamond in my fist, I've tried to
hold a candle to the sun. And all through
the long corridor of my sleep I tossed
and yearned and dreamed a woman in a yellow
skirt. And she was always singing. How
the spiral stairway we travel on, is only
a burning thing.

I live in a garage with a shrine while the
rain is streaming down the window pane and
my heart's on the mend. Though I've gone
to hell and back in a birchbark canoe and
have died ten times since eight o'clock
this morning. And remember a kiss in a
taxi once as we drove right over the falls.

With a leaf from the south in my hair
and a heart that beat and beat, while
I told it all and exhumed my shadow
while the night air was inhaling me
and a flower bloomed on my skin. And
later that path that led up the mountain
where it was the wisdom of emptiness.
A bird in the rosebush. The river in
June. O like a boy on a dolphin, I
waved one hand at the sea

I say awake and I awaken to the
possibility of light. To the idea
of your hand upon my skin. Or a
kiss like a burning flower on my
lips. When our hearts are just
crisp roots of the earth and we're
into the business of being. And
later the moonlight will suckle the
lily as the ladybug crosses the screen.

A death and a resurrection all in the
space of an inch. Where somewhere in
my neighbourhood I'm lost and found
again. And feel the pulse and urge to
phone and call the sky a miracle. Like
young Horatio, who just lay down in the
darkness and had his first glimpse of
ecstasy. O we're here brother. We're
here on the turning earth.

It was the name I gave the darkness
and the grass fire in my mind that
made me think we verge toward the edge.
Though my emptiness is not my depletion
and I'm going deep as a star in a well.
And will mold the clay in my fingers
into the shape of a burning man. And
who knows. Maybe the dead do sing
and that is what we hear. While the
world unfurls beneath us like a wing.

When all that remains is to do one gracious
thing. Like simply name who you are in the
April light. Or dance with a wild iris
as a white lace curtain blows into an empty room.
For once you've entered the labyrinth
and named the night within, you can hear the ribald
laughter of that fiddle in the wings. Knowing
then which road to take. All the way home.

I was watching Alexandra read her book.
There by the mirror of the water, with a
wind that strummed a note in her ear.
Then marking her place with a fallen leaf
she whistles for the pizza man. And I
come running, ringing the tinker's bell.
Thinking this could be the night when we'll
murder a tango. Across all the rooftops
of the world.

It was there by a rushing stream
where I learned to bow, as graciously
as water over stone. So I'm opening
to diamonds and light. I'm opening to
time and its arrow and the thing that
makes the sky tick. Where I tear a
page out of the Bible and fold it
into a paper dart.
      O a skydiver with a nose-bleed
I hurl toward the burning earth.

It's like a favorite record that you own
that you play over and over. I'm talking
about the circular heart. The thing that
has worn its own groove into the solid
earth. And goes on sometimes like a Maypole
with a dozen streaming ribbons. The thing
that aches and the thing that sings about
the star's reflection on the blue lagoon.
O sometimes the heart says no. Then, its
eternal yes. While the night goes on like
a burning wing and lights appear on the
coast. While I'm checking out the back seat
to see if you are there.

It's what I did to save the world, I
simply lit a candle and tied a silk bow
onto the sleeve of sorrow. When the
night unfurled its ribbon and everything
rang in me. O it wasn't that easy
inventing those seabirds and all the
cries that they made in the air. While
dead men on the avenue are hoping to
transform their sleep into the chants
and kisses of the young.

It was just the nightwind in the trees while
I went through tangled streets that echoed
like an argument. Toward some arch I'd known
once under which the birds had flown. I the
eternal vagabond, bequeathing you this fragment
of the sky. For the world is no illusion is
what I wrote in sand. Standing there, near the
edge, immersed in the going-round. Somewhere
between a thicket and a star.

So I've swept the blue rug and found my own
salvation in my arms. Then say my prayer and
mantra as a whole world opens up. What might
be there then, what I might lean towards
to burn like any passion in the rain. For a
bright light burns in a dark age and I'm here
dreaming light. Dreaming clothes on a line.
When time all those years rang like a bell in
my skin. O like all the saints, I've believed
in wings and gone the rocky distance with a hymn.
With a mind like a river
and a heart
like a torch.

I see her statue in the Cathedral yard every time
I walk to the candle store. The Virgin Mary. In
the statue she is standing with her head slightly
bowed and her arms at her sides with the palms of
her hands facing forward. And do you know what I
am going to tell you. I feel sometimes that the
Virgin Mary looks out for me. And some nights I
even feel her presence in my room. And have always
thought that she would understand me in a way
that Jesus never could.

In a way we're all on death-row and that
is why we sing. Can you hear my aria in
the alley. I who have nothing, yet
everything, if you know what I mean. O
among the wounded I am known as a beauty.
So it's Oriental thinking and the sound
of a chime. When some song I thought I'd
never sing is filling up the lane. Where
I'm waving the bones on Paradise Street.
And have learned to kiss the dark.

Grateful then for these small aches and the
night that keeps me humble. While I try to
decipher the meaning of things. Like a man
who went to the edge of ruin while the sky
bloomed in every tree and two birds sang.
Like a brief moment in the summer rain with
three coins and a kid in the fountain. For
it's only the diamond in the mind. The thing
I knew when the thrush called and a sign was
revealed to me. When the darkest night I ever
knew became my greatest blessing.